Crabapples

Wings, Wheels & Sails

Bobbie Kalman

🌱 Crabtree Publishing Company

Crabapples

created by Bobbie Kalman

for baby Michael

Editor-in-Chief
Bobbie Kalman

Writing team
Bobbie Kalman
Petrina Gentile
David Schimpky

Managing editor
Lynda Hale

Editors
Tammy Everts
Lynda Hale

Computer design
Lynda Hale
David Schimpky

Illustrations
Barb Bedell: pages 9, 22, 24
Jeannette McNaughton: pages 14, 23, 27, back cover
Debra Watton: page 21

Color separations and film
Dot 'n Line Image Inc.

Printer
Worzalla Publishing Company

Special thanks to
Rob Turner at C&C International, Randy Garrett and Simon Drakefort, India Tourist Organization, Japan Information Center, Kennedy Space Center, the staff of Ed Learn Ford, Greg St. Amand, Jerry Ungaro of Downtown Limo, and Dave Walsh at the University of Waterloo

Photographs
David Barbour/CIDA: page 30
C&C International: page 8
Marc Crabtree: page 5 (bottom left)
Patrick H. Davies: page 11 (top)
Winston Fraser: pages 14, 20 (top)
T. Freda/Visual Contact: page 16 (top left)
Petrina Gentile: page 24
Heather Halfyard: pages 5 (top), 26 (bottom), 26-27 (top)
India Tourist Organization: page 6
Japan Information Center: pages 20-21 (bottom)
Bobbie Kalman: pages 10 (bottom), 15 (bottom), 19 (top), 23 (bottom)
Kennedy Space Center: pages 28-29
Jerome Knap: page 7 (bottom)
Molly Lawson: page 5 (bottom right)
W. Lowry/Visual Contact: page 25 (top)
Diane Payton Majumdar: page 4 (top)
Ontario Ministry of the Environment: page 18 (top)
Alese & Mort Pechter: pages 12, 13
Steven Pedretti: pages 4 (bottom right), 15 (middle)
W. Randall/Visual Contact: page 25 (bottom)
Janine Schaub: title page, page 31
David Schimpky: pages 16 (middle left, bottom left), 18 (bottom), 19 (bottom)
Mike Silver: page 11 (bottom)
Lydia Tenke: page 15 (top)
Ken Tinker: pages 7 (top), 10 (top)
University of Waterloo, Department of Systems Design: front cover, page 17
Berndt Wegener: page 16 (top right)

Crabtree Publishing Company

350 Fifth Avenue
Suite 3308
New York
N.Y. 10118

360 York Road, RR 4,
Niagara-on-the-Lake,
Ontario, Canada
L0S 1J0

73 Lime Walk
Headington
Oxford OX3 7AD
United Kingdom

Cataloging in Publication Data
Kalman, Bobbie, 1947-
    Wings, wheels, and sails

(Crabapples)
Includes index.

ISBN 0-86505-608-0 (library bound)   ISBN 0-86505-708-7 (pbk.)
This book looks at the different ways of traveling on land, in water, and in the sky.

1. Transportation - Juvenile literature. 2. Vehicles - Juvenile literature. I. Title. II. Series: Kalman, Bobbie, 1947-
Crabapples.

TA1149.K35 1995   j629.046   LC 94-43539
                                                                   CIP

M5658

What is in this book?

Getting around

People go from place to place every day. They go to work, to school, and to visit their friends. Some people travel to faraway places. Others go just down the street.

Using different ways to get from here to there is called **transportation**. Airplanes, cars, bicycles, trains, and sailboats are some methods of transportation.

When we travel by plane, wings help the airplane stay in the air. When we ride a bicycle, use in-line skates, or drive a car, wheels take us where we want to go. Sails on a sailboat catch the wind and move the boat across the water.

Wings, wheels, and sails are not the only ways we travel. Name some other ways people get around. What is your favorite way of traveling?

Animal helpers

A long time ago, walking was the only way people could travel. Long journeys were very tiring and could take weeks or months. People soon learned that some animals could be trained to carry them and their belongings.

In many countries, animals still help people move from place to place. Some people ride elephants. The rider sits behind the animal's head. The elephants sometimes have beautiful designs painted on their heads and bodies. In Asia, people use elephants to carry heavy loads. The elephants haul logs out of the forest.

Horses are popular all over the world. They are easy to ride and can pull wagons and carts of all kinds. Donkeys and llamas are sure-footed. They can carry people and goods over rough ground in mountain areas.

Camels are sometimes called "ships of the desert." They can go for a month without water.

Dog teams pull sleds across the snowy Arctic. In very cold weather, the dogs wear leather slippers to protect their feet.

Ships ahoy!

If you want to be a sailor,
Here are some names you'll have to learn.
The front of the boat is called the **bow**,
And the back is called the **stern**.

The **tiller** moves the **rudder**.
The rudder steers the boat.
The **mast** holds up the **mainsail**,
And the **hull** keeps it afloat.

If you go into the **cabin**,
You'll see cupboards, shelves,
  and beds.
The kitchen is called
  the **galley**,
And the toilet is the **head**!

mast

mainsail

tiller

stern

bow

hull

rudder

9

Making waves

Some boats and ships have sails, but many do not. They have engines. The engine turns a propeller, which pushes the boat through the water.

A cruise ship is a moving hotel. It has restaurants, stores, and hundreds of rooms. Many cruise ships even have swimming pools and movie theaters.

A hydrofoil is a boat with underwater wings called **foils**. When a hydrofoil goes very fast, its hull rises out of the water. Hydrofoils can skim over water faster than other kinds of boats.

Ferries take people across rivers, lakes, and some parts of the ocean. They are powered by motors or towed by cables. Some ferries carry only passengers. Others carry cars and even trains!

Under the water

Submarines, such as the one below, can travel beneath the sea. When a submarine "dives" into the ocean, sea water rushes into large tanks on board. The water makes the submarine so heavy that it sinks. When the water is let out of the tanks, the submarine rises.

Submersibles are small submarines that can dive very deep. They can get into tight places, even cracks on the ocean floor. Submersibles are often used by scientists who study the deepest parts of the ocean.

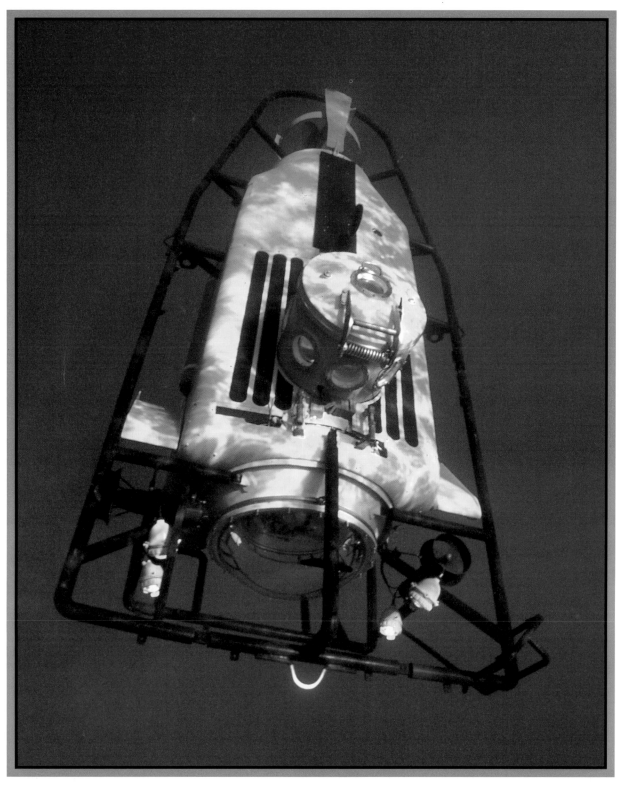

The wheel

Before the wheel

Early wheel

spoke

A wheel with spokes

Can you imagine life without wheels? There would be no wagons, bicycles, cars, or in-line skates. Almost every kind of land transportation uses wheels.

Wheels have changed a lot since they were first invented. They can be made of many different materials. Plastic skateboard wheels roll easily on pavement. Knobby rubber tires help dirt bikes move on bumpy trails. Some wheels are big and light and float on water. Wheels are both useful and fun!

Cars, cars, cars

There is a car to suit every kind of person. Sports cars are for people who like to go fast. Limousines are for people who want to travel in style. Some people enjoy a windy ride in a convertible. Others like big cars that have plenty of room. Which of these cars is your favorite?

A car's engine turns the wheels and makes the car move. To run, engines need fuel. Most cars use gasoline as fuel. Some cars use natural gas.

Solar cars use the energy of the sun's rays. The sun's energy is turned into electricity. Using the energy of the sun, the solar car shown below can run for nine hours. It does not create pollution the way a car that runs on gasoline does. Scientists are working hard to make solar cars run faster and longer.

Wheels at work

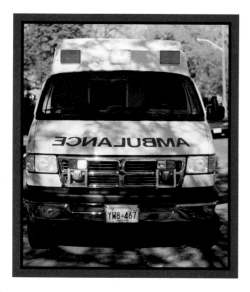

Our communities are full of trucks. Trucks are made to do hard work! Garbage trucks keep towns and cities clean. Ambulances and fire trucks save lives. Buses carry passengers from place to place.

Pickup trucks and vans carry light loads. Dump trucks and cement mixers are used in building houses and roads.

Transport trucks pull huge trailers. Some transports have a bed behind the seat where the driver can rest during a long trip.

Riding the rails

Trains, streetcars, and subways have small wheels that run on steel rails or tracks. Their engines use diesel fuel or electricity.

Streetcars travel city streets. They make many stops to pick up passengers. Subways move under the ground. They allow people to travel from place to place underneath busy cities.

Monorails are trains that run on one rail instead of two. The track is built high above the ground. Wide wheels keep the cars on the rail.

The train below is called a **bullet train** because it travels very fast. Powered by electricity, it travels over special rails. **Maglev trains** do not have wheels! They use the power of magnets to move above a rail. These trains can travel at very high speeds.

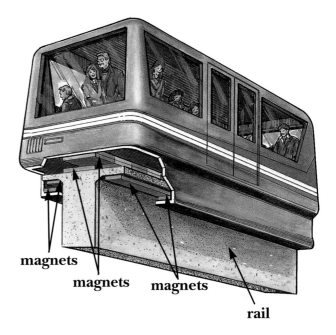

magnets

magnets   magnets

rail

The first fliers

Before airplanes were invented, people tried to fly in different ways. Some attached huge wings of wood and cloth to their arms and jumped from a high place. Although they flapped their wings as quickly as they could, they always crashed!

Wilbur and Orville Wright were the first people to fly an airplane. They used a car engine to keep their plane in the air. The flight took place at Kitty Hawk, North Carolina, in 1903.

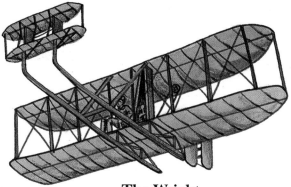

The Wright brothers' airplane

After the Wright brothers took off, other people started building and flying airplanes. These old airplanes do not look much like the jet airplanes of today!

An Italian airplane from 1909

A French airplane from 1909

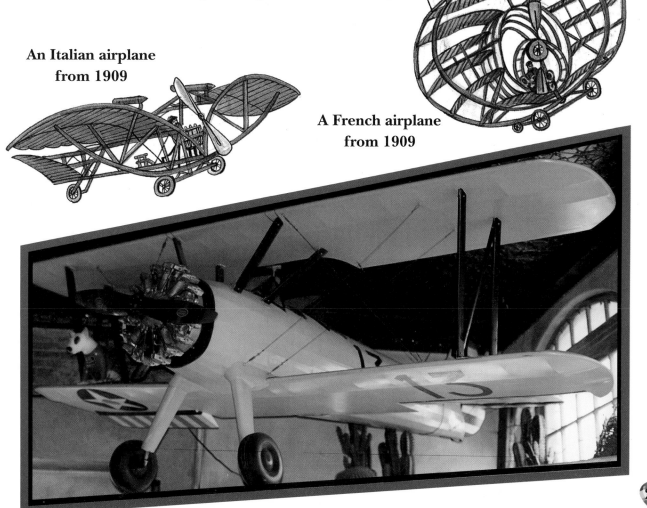

Winging it!

Lift and **thrust** allow airplanes to fly. The air moving under the wings lifts the plane up. The engines thrust the plane forward. Unless lift and thrust work together, the plane will not get off the ground.

The pilot sits in the cockpit of the plane. There are many dials, switches, and knobs in the cockpit. It takes many years to learn how to fly a plane.

Moving flaps help the airplane move up, down, right, and left.

flap

jet engines

flap

jet engines

A helicopter has a huge propeller on top that lifts it above the ground. It can fly forwards, backwards, up, down, and sideways. Helicopters can even hover in the air.

Gliders do not have engines. They are made of lightweight materials. To take off, a glider is pulled into the sky by an airplane. When the plane lets it go, the glider soars on its own.

Up, up, and away!

Air is all around us. We cannot see it, but warm air rises above cool air. Balloons use hot air to rise up into the sky. The air inside the huge bag is heated with fire. The bag is made of thin, strong material. Passengers ride in a basket that hangs below the balloon.

The Montgolfier brothers, two French scientists, invented the first balloon. It was made of cloth and paper. A sheep, a duck, and a rooster were the first passengers to ride in the balloon. They traveled 17 meters (57 feet) up into the air.

3...2...1... Blast off!

A **spacecraft** is a vehicle that travels in space. Most spacecraft can be used only once, but a space shuttle can make many trips into space.

To lift off, the shuttle needs lots of power. **Booster rockets** help the **main engines** lift the shuttle into the sky. The **external tank** provides extra fuel for the main engines. The tank and the booster rockets fall off when the fuel is gone. The shuttle returns to earth without them.

SPACE SHUTTLE

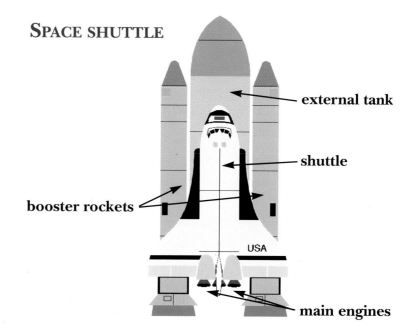

external tank

shuttle

booster rockets

USA

main engines

Changing the way we move

Transportation helps us get from place to place, but many ways of traveling hurt the earth. Cars and trucks are especially harmful because their engines create air pollution.

Scientists are working to design better car engines. Many cars now have **catalytic converters**, which help clean the harmful gases that engines create.

When people use public transportation there are fewer cars on the road. Buses, subways, streetcars, and trains can move lots of people at once. Bicycles and in-line skates create no pollution at all. They are also a great way to get exercise!

Words to know

Arctic The cold region around the north pole

catalytic converter A device that cleans gases from a car engine

convertible A car with a roof that folds down

foil A small wing beneath a hydrofoil

fuel Something that is burned to make an engine work

llama A South American animal related to the camel

monorail A train that moves along a single rail

natural gas A type of fuel

propeller Turning blades that move some boats and airplanes

solar Describing something that is related to the sun

Index

1 2 3 4 5 6 7 8 9 0 Printed in USA 4 3 2 1 0 9 8 7 6 5